Olivier & Danielle Föllmi

Offerings

SPIRITUAL WISDOM TO CHANGE YOUR LIFE

Buddha Shakyamuni - Pema Chödrön - His Holiness the 14th Dalai Lama - Arnaud Desjardins -
Dilgo Khyentse Rinpoche - Dudjom Rinpoche - Joseph Goldstein - Lama Anagarika Govinda -
Kalu Rinpoche - Jack Kornfield - Milarepa - Matthieu Ricard - Sharon Salzberg -
Shabkar - Shantideva - Sogyal Rinpoche - Chögyam Trungpa

Stewart, Tabori & Chang
New York

To Tenzin Motup, Tenzin Diskit, Nyima Lhamo,

A little town on the arid plains of India, Bodhgaya is the most sacred place in Buddhism. In January 2002, sitting cross-legged around the tree beneath which Buddha reached Enlightenment, thousands of monks in their red robes chanted prayers for world peace. All around them, three hundred thousand pilgrims who had come down from all the valleys of the Himalayas chanted with them, prayer beads in hand. It was here, in front of the tree of Buddha, in the overwhelming fervour of this enormous choir, that the concept of this book came into being: to let this wish for peace shine out from every one of us.

Tharpa Tsenring and Pema Yangdun, our Tibetan children

This is a collection of messages from the masters of Tibetan Buddhism, from different schools and different eras, and the thoughts of the Western disciples that have been inspired by their teachings. Each week is covered by one of fifty-two themes, the causes of suffering, the development of the individual, the couple, the family, society and humanity as a whole. Each week ends meditatively on a double-page image. The images in this book reflect the richness and diversity of the Buddhist Himalayas, from Tibet, India, Bhutan and Nepal.
May this book be of aid to every one of us on the path to Enlightenment.

Danielle and Olivier Föllmi

*O*ne doesn't take a journey into the Himalayas
without a guide who knows the ancient paths.

Jack Kornfield

It is not easy to be reborn as a human being. It is rarer than for a one-eyed turtle, who rises to the surface only once every hundred years, to push his neck through a wooden yoke with one hole that floats on the surface of the wide ocean.

Buddha Shakyamuni

Hear me! In our future lives it will be hard to regain this precious human state, with all its privileges and freedoms. The moment of our death is impossible to predict. Who can say? Perhaps we will die tonight.

Shabkar

Life is fragile, like the dew hanging delicately on the grass,
crystal drops that will be carried away on the first morning breeze.

Dilgo Khyentse Rinpoche

We will never again have the chance to be born into a body like this one.

Kalu Rinpoche

When shall I encounter once again an incarnate Buddha,
faith, human existence, and the ability to practice virtue,
all of these things so difficult to find?

Shantideva

Let us try to recognize the precious nature of each day.

The 14th Dalai Lama

8 January

Like the birds that gather in the treetops at night
And scatter in all directions at the coming of dawn,
Phenomena are impermanent.

Shabkar

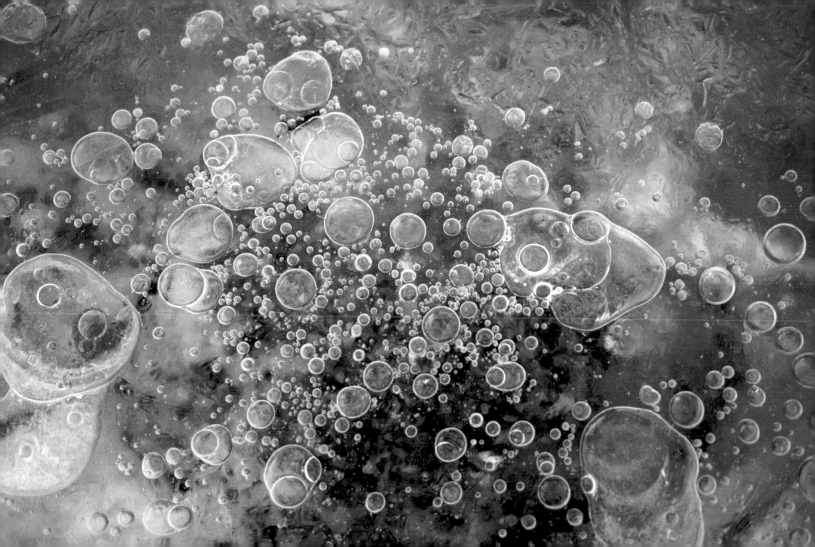

Nothing is permanent:
The sun and the moon rise and then set,
The bright, clear day is followed by the deep, dark night.
From hour to hour, everything changes.

Kalu Rinpoche

Impermanence is a principle of harmony. When we don't struggle against it, we are in harmony with reality.

Pema Chödrön

Suzuki Roshi summed up all the teachings of Buddhism in three simple words: 'Not always so.'

Jack Kornfield

12 January

To take for permanent
That which is only transitory
Is like the delusion of a madman.

Kalu Rinpoche

Awareness of impermanence is encouraged, so that when it is coupled with our appreciation of the enormous potential of our human existence, it will give us a sense of urgency that I must use every precious moment.

The 14th Dalai Lama

Just as a traveller on a journey takes lodging,
a being who travels the cycle of existence takes lodging in a rebirth.

Shantideva

This tool, our body, is given to us for only a short time: this life.

Dilgo Khyentse Rinpoche

Like a robe wears out over time and turns to rags,
life wears out from day to day, from second to second.

Dilgo Khyentse Rinpoche

Our lives are like an hourglass that never stops…
Each moment follows the one before, without end.
From moment to moment, life drains away:
We are babies, then adults, then old and dead,
Each moment follows the one before, without end.
Our lives are like a bubble or a candle;
Impermanence and death are like the wind!

Kalu Rinpoche

Letting go is a central theme in spiritual practice,
as we see the preciousness and brevity of life.

Jack Kornfield

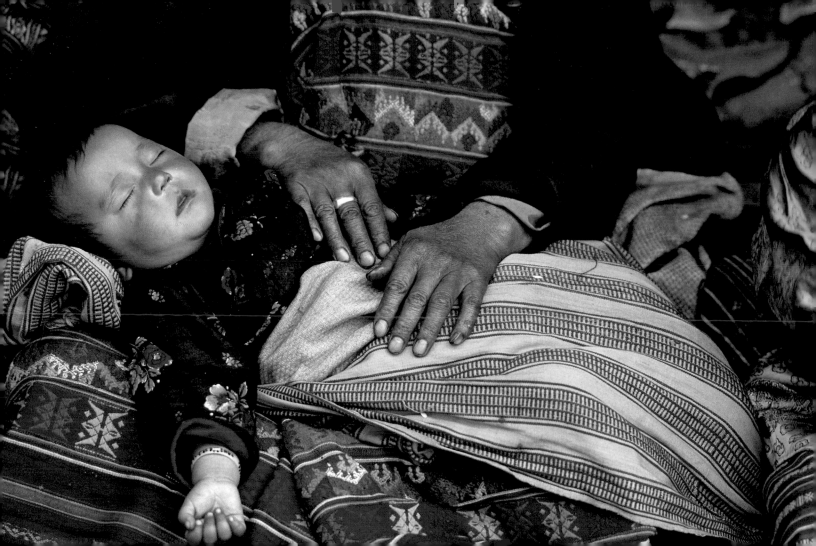

Why, if we are as pragmatic as we claim,
don't we begin to ask ourselves seriously:
Where does our real *future lie?*

Sogyal Rinpoche

You see, we are all dying. It's only a matter of time.
Some of us just die sooner than others.

Dudjom Rinpoche

On the day that you were born, you began to die.

Do not waste a single moment more!

Dilgo Khyentse Rinpoche

Come back to square one, just the minimum bare bones.
Relaxing with the present moment, relaxing with hopelessness, relaxing with death,
not resisting the fact that things end, that things pass, that things have no lasting substance,
that everything is changing all the time — that is the basic message.

Pema Chödrön

Death is neither depressing nor exciting; it is simply a fact of life.

Sogyal Rinpoche

Terrible or not, difficult or not, the only thing that is beautiful,
noble, religious and mystical is to be happy.

Arnaud Desjardins

I ask myself why we do not practise,

just for those few moments of time in which death has lent us our bodies.

Dilgo Khyentse Rinpoche

If you do not make good use of this free and precious life,
What good does it do to possess a human body?

Shabkar

We must make good use of this life for the time that we have left,
This brief flash of light, like the sun appearing through the clouds.

Kalu Rinpoche

Fulfilling spiritual life can never come through imitation,
it must shine through our particular gifts and capacities
as a man or woman on this earth. This is the pearl of great price.

Jack Kornfield

In honouring our own unique destiny,
we allow our most personal life to become an expression of the Buddha in a new form.

Jack Kornfield

Every individual in the world has a unique contribution.

Jack Kornfield

The first thing upon which we should meditate
Is our precious and fleeting human life,
Hard to obtain, and easy to destroy;
I will now give it meaning.

Kalu Rinpoche

When we respect the natural cycles of life,
we find that each of life's stages has a spiritual dimension.

Jack Kornfield

One of the major sources of our spiritual consciousness is found in our earliest life —
the benevolent oneness of existence in our mother's womb. Then, as an infant,
we experience the freshness of seeing, feeling and touching the world for the first time,
the immediate physical presence of our senses and our own needs. Reawakening this intimacy,
recapturing a spontaneous unbroken trust in what we know and feel,
is essential to finding our spiritual ground in later practice.

Jack Kornfield

Many people have their first spiritual experience in childhood,
that of an innate and natural connection with what is sacred and holy.
The playfulness, joy and curiosity of our childhood can become a foundation
for the delighted rediscovery of this spirit in our practice. If our relationship
with our parents is respectful and loving, that too becomes a model
and foundation for respect and trust in all other relationships.

Jack Kornfield

The independence and rebelliousness of our adolescence offer us yet another quality essential to our practice: the insistence that we find out the truth for ourselves, accepting no one's word above our own experience.

Jack Kornfield

Adult life brings its own natural spiritual tasks and openings.
We become more caring and responsible for our family, our community, our world.
We discover the need for vision and feel a strong desire to fulfil our own unique expression of life.
As we mature, a natural contemplative quality enters our life. We can sense a movement within
to seek periods of reflection and to gain perspective, to stay in touch with our heart.

Jack Kornfield

As we age, having seen many cycles of birth and death,
there is a detachment and a wisdom that grows within us.

Jack Kornfield

From the very day of our birth, when we drink our mother's milk,
compassion arises within us. This act is a symbol of love and affection. I think this act,
from the very first day of life, establishes the basis for our entire life.

The 14th Dalai Lama

*Only the proper environmental conditions are required to allow
the underlying and natural 'seed of compassion' to germinate and grow.*

Howard Cutler

Education should be in harmony with the child's essentially kind nature.
The most important element is that children be raised in a climate of love and tenderness.
Although from an ideal perspective human qualities ought to be developed in conjunction with kindness,
I often say that if I had to choose between important general qualities and kindness,
I believe I would choose kindness.

The 14th Dalai Lama

The true essence of humankind is kindness. There are other qualities which come from education or knowledge, but it is essential, if one wishes to be a genuine human being and impart satisfying meaning to one's existence, to have a good heart.

The 14th Dalai Lama

To think of the immense wall of potential hidden deep within our being,
to understand that the nature of mind is fundamental purity and kindness,
and to meditate on its luminosity, will enable you to develop self-confidence and courage.

The 14th Dalai Lama

We can awaken to basic goodness, our birthright.

Pema Chödrön

Who am I? Who is carrying this body?

Jack Kornfield

The mind produces a powerful illusion,
that of existing in this body which we consider to be our own.

Kalu Rinpoche

*We see that life, composed of this mind and body, is in a state of
continual constant transformation and flux. There is always the possibility
of radical change. Every moment — not just poetically or figuratively, but literally —
every moment we are dying and being reborn, we and all of life.*

Sharon Salzberg

The Buddha described us as a collection of five changing processes:
the processes of the physical body, of feelings, of perceptions, of responses,
and of the flow of consciousness that experiences them all.
Our sense of self arises whenever we grasp at or identify with these patterns.
Our world and sense of self is a play of patterns. Any identity
we can grasp is transient, tentative.

Jack Kornfield

Perhaps the deepest reason why we are afraid of death is because we do not know who we are.
We believe in a personal, unique and separate identity; but if we dare to examine it,
we find that this identity depends entirely on an endless collection of things to prop it up;
our name, our 'biography', our partners, family, home, job, friends, credit cards…
It is on their fragile and transient support that we rely for our security.

Sogyal Rinpoche

When we examine our body, word and mind, we try in vain
to find anything permanent there. The concept of an individual person
is only sane and valid if we consider it to be one single aspect of global interdependence.

Matthieu Ricard

Whether we regard our situation as heaven or as hell depends on our perception.

Pema Chödrön

Our five senses are like openings through which we receive all the perceptions that are then transformed into concepts and ideas.

Arnaud Desjardins

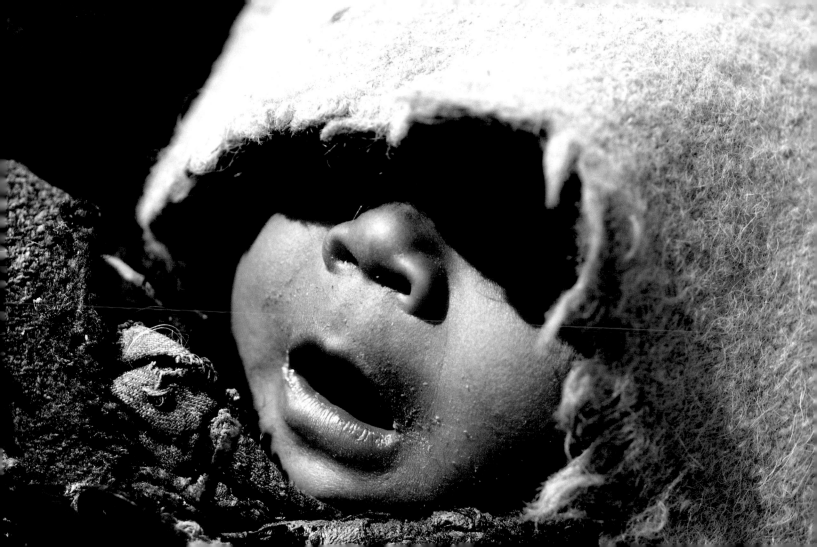

Confidence is closely linked to how well our perceptions match reality.

Matthieu Ricard

Peace of mind is rooted in affection and compassion.
There is a very high level of sensitivity and feeling there.

The 14th Dalai Lama

A bridge is revealed which connects the everyday temporal world of sense perceptions to the realm of timeless knowledge.

Lama Anagarika Govinda

To see the preciousness of all things, we must bring our full attention to life.

Jack Kornfield

Our consciousness contains all these roles and more,
the hero and the lover, the hermit, the dictator, the wise woman and the fool.

Jack Kornfield

Do not take lightly small good deeds,
Believing they can hardly help.
For drops of water, one by one,
In time can fill a giant pot.

Patrul Rinpoche

We are the sum of a huge number of free actions for which we are the only ones responsible.

Matthieu Ricard and Trinh Xuan Thuan

8 March

Actions may be positive or negative according to the intention that underlies them,

just as a crystal refracts the colours of its surroundings.

Dilgo Khyentse Rinpoche

*The better we understand the nature of mind, the more deeply we will be able to see
into the endless chain of cause and effect that is karma. This understanding not only allows us to avoid
or reduce the negative actions which harm others or ourselves and the suffering caused by these,
but also lets us cultivate and increase positive actions which create well-being and happiness.*

Kalu Rinpoche

It is only through constant training that our practice will grow steady and we will be able to control our negative tendencies fearlessly.

Dilgo Khyentse Rinpoche

Our actions, our words and our thoughts determine our karma,
in other words, the happiness and the suffering that will be our lot.

Dilgo Khyentse Rinpoche

We are all slaves of our own actions. Why be angry with anyone else?

Shantideva

When we feel responsible, concerned and committed,
we begin to feel deep emotion and great courage.

The 14th Dalai Lama

Each individual is master of his or her destiny:
it is up to each person to create the causes of happiness.

The 14th Dalai Lama

Happiness is the result of inner maturity. It depends on us alone, and requires patient work, carried out from day to day. Happiness must be built, and this requires time and effort. In the long term, happiness and unhappiness are therefore a way of being, or a life skill.

Matthieu Ricard

If there are obstacles, it cannot be space,

If there are numbers, it cannot be stars,

If it moves and shakes, it cannot be a mountain,

If it grows and shrinks, it cannot be an ocean,

If it must be crossed by a bridge, it cannot be a river,

If it can be grasped, it cannot be a rainbow.

These are the six parables of outer perception.

Milarepa

*We can bring an open and respectful attention
to the sensations that make up our bodily experience.*

Jack Kornfield

If we knew that tonight we were going to go blind,
we would take a longing, last *real look at every blade of grass, every cloud formation,*
every speck of dust, every rainbow, raindrop — everything.

Pema Chödrön

Touch is the vehicle through which we comfort one another and are comforted, via hugs or clasps of the hand.

Howard Cutler

The things that matter most in our lives are not fantastic or grand.

They are the moments when we touch one another.

Jack Kornfield

The body and the word have great importance:
it is through their support that the true nature of mind can be realized.
It could be said that, in a way, the body and the word are the servants of the mind.

Kalu Rinpoche

བདག་དང་སྐྱོ་ནི་ལག་ག་ཅིག་ཏུ་ཤུག
བདག་ལགས་པར་འདུག་པ་ཏྲི་ཉེ་ག་ལུ་པོ
གལང་ཁ་ཕ་སྐྲུ་དང་ནར་གཅུ་སྐྱ་ནབ
ལ་དུ་ག་ཅུ་ཟ་དུང་པ་ར་ཉིག
ག་གི་ལུ་ནས་པ་ང་ཡ་དང་ཨེ
ཁ་ཡུལ་ཞིག་ན་མོ་ང་བ་ཉི་མ་ནོང
ཁ་ནས་ཞ་ཧ་ག་ཅུ་ད་ངཱ་ནི
བ་ས་ཉེ་ཁ་ཅི་དང་བ་ཉ་ང་པ་ཀུ་ཏུ
ཁ་ཉི་ཁ་ང་ལ་ཡ་ང་ཆི་ད་བ་ཆུ
ཀྱི་ཝ་ས་མ་ག་ཉི་ད་ར་པ་ཉི་ཚོ་ཆ

རང་། །ཡེ་ཤེས་དབང་ཀ་ན་ཆེ་མེ་ད་ར་བཞིན་

ཆུང་ཆེན་ཤིག །ཧུ་ལ་གཏིང་ཀ་ཡི་ཝ་ཧ་ལ་སྟེ།

ཞིང་དུ་མས་ཀ། །ཞེ་ར་ར་བས་མ་ཆི་ན་མེ

ཁ་ར་ན་ལ་ཆུ་ན་དུ་མས། །ཁ་ང་ལ་ཆུ་

མུ་ཤ་ཆེ་དུ་མ་ན་བཞུ་ག་ན་པ་ཨཱ། །ཁུ་སྟ

ཤུར་ལ་སྦྱེ་ཅེ་བལ་ན་ར་ཨཽ། །ར་ཁྲ

མ་སུ་ལ་ ཐམས་ཆད་ཁྱིག་ལ་སུ་ལ་པ།

མུ་ཆེ་མ་ཁེ་ལ་དུ་ན་ག་ལུ་ཆེ། །ཤེ་ར་ཞི

བ་ས་མ་ཆུ་ན་ཆུ་མཆེ་ཞེ་ར་ར་མ་ན་ཆུ་

བ་མ་ལ་དཆུ་མཆེ་ར་སྐྲི་ཏི་ཏ་ཝ་བ་ཐུ་

ག་ཁུ་ན་ཆེ་ཀ་ཡ་ཀ་ལ་ན་ཆུ་མཆེ་ཞི་སྦྱ་ཀ།

Aggressive words damage and hurt others. They can be thrown in someone else's face, or hidden among jokes; they can even mean telling friends their faults to their faces. The result of these actions is a scorching, arid and thorny environment.

Kalu Rinpoche

*Unfortunately, we do not recognize the empty nature of words
and we become fixated on them as if they were something real. This is why
pleasant words make us happy, and unpleasant words make us unhappy
or angry. These reactions are a sign that we believe in the reality of words.*

Kalu Rinpoche.

Not causing harm requires staying awake.
Part of being awake is slowing down enough to notice what we say and do.
The more we witness our emotional chain reactions and understand how they work,
the easier it is to refrain. It becomes a way of life to stay awake,
slow down, and notice.

Pema Chödrön

When one intends to move or speak,
one should first examine one's own mind
and then act appropriately with composure.

Shantideva

Words should be coherent and controlled,
clear and pleasant, and should be spoken in a calm and gentle voice;
they should express neither desire nor hatred.

Shantideva

Of the ten virtuous acts spoken of in Buddhism,
four are verbal: do not lie, defame others, speak offensive words,
or engage in frivolous conversation.

The 14th Dalai Lama

The ordinary mind is the ceaselessly shifting and shiftless prey of external influences, habitual tendencies, and conditioning; the masters liken it to a candle flame in an open doorway, vulnerable to all the winds of circumstance.

Sogyal Rinpoche

We live under threat from painful emotions: anger, desire, pride, jealousy and so on.
Therefore we should always be ready to counter these with the appropriate antidote.
True practitioners may be recognized by their unfailing mindfulness.

Dilgo Khyentse Rinpoche

It is the place of feeling that binds us or frees us.

Jack Kornfield

*It is by striving ceaselessly to change our emotions
that we will succeed in changing our temperament.*

Matthieu Ricard

6 April

One who strives to attain Enlightenment must expect to encounter terrible obstacles: anger, desire, mental confusion, pride and jealousy.

Dilgo Khyentse Rinpoche

Instead of allowing ourselves to be led and trapped by our feelings,
we should let them disappear as soon as they form, like letters drawn on water with a finger.

Dilgo Khyentse Rinpoche

Until we stop clinging to the concept of good and evil,
the world will continue to manifest as friendly goddesses and harmful demons.

Pema Chödrön

Passions do not exist in objects, nor in the senses, nor in the space between, nor anywhere else. Then where are they, that they torment the whole world? They are nothing but illusions. So, my heart, leave behind your fear, and strive towards wisdom. Why should you put yourself through hell for no reason?

Shantideva

See demons as demons: that is the danger.

Know that they are powerless: that is the way.

Understand them for what they are: that is deliverance.

Recognize them as your father and mother: that is their end.

Realize that they are creations of the mind: they become its glory.

When these truths are known, all is liberation.

Milarepa

The basic root of happiness lies in our minds;
outer circumstances are nothing more than adverse or favourable.

Matthieu Ricard

The real world is beyond our thoughts and ideas; we see it through the net of our desires, divided into pleasure and pain, right and wrong, inner and outer. To see the universe as it is, you must step beyond the net. It is not hard to do, for the net is full of holes.

Sri Nisargadatta

16 April

The mind in its natural state can be compared to the sky,
covered by layers of cloud which hide its true nature.

Kalu Rinpoche

We live a form of false perception of reality.

Matthieu Ricard

Do not encumber your mind with useless thoughts.

What good does it do to brood on the past or anticipate the future?

Remain in the simplicity of the present moment.

Dilgo Khyentse Rinpoche

Reaching a state of inner freedom as regards emotions does not mean being apathetic or insensitive,
nor does it mean that existence loses its colour in the slightest. It simply means that,
instead of always being the plaything of our negative thoughts, moods,
and temperaments, we become their masters.

Matthieu Ricard

Achieving genuine happiness may require bringing about a transformation in your outlook, your way of thinking, and this is not a simple matter.

The 14th Dalai Lama

We can bring our spiritual practice into the streets, into our communities,
when we see each realm as a temple, as a place to discover that which is sacred.

Jack Kornfield

If one were truly aware of the value of human life, to waste it blithely on distractions and the pursuit of vulgar ambitions would be the height of confusion.

Dilgo Khyentse Rinpoche

The only source of blame is the confusion that reigns in our minds,
a chaos which Buddhism calls ignorance.

Matthieu Ricard

The mind is restless, unsteady,
hard to guard, hard to control.
The wise one makes it straight,
like a fletcher straightens an arrow.

How good it is to rein the mind
Which is unruly, capricious, rushing wherever it pleases.
The mind so harnessed will bring one happiness.

Your worst enemy cannot harm you
as much as your own unguarded thoughts.
A well-directed mind creates more happiness
Than even the loving actions of your parents.

Buddha Shakyamuni, quoted by Joseph Goldstein

To exercise right mindfulness, the mind must be neither too taut,
nor too relaxed, like the string of a vina.

Kalu Rinpoche

The more sophisticated the level of our knowledge is,
the more effective we will be in dealing with the natural world.

The 14th Dalai Lama

Knowledge does not mean mastering a great quantity of different information, but understanding the nature of mind. This knowledge can penetrate each one of our thoughts and illuminate each one of our perceptions.

Matthieu Ricard

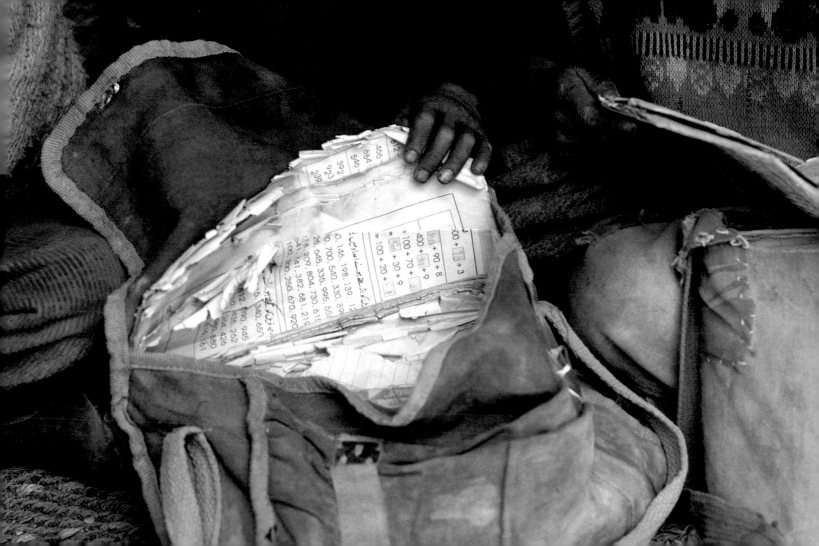

Somehow, in the process of trying to deny that things are always changing, we lose our sense of the sacredness of life. We tend to forget that we are part of the natural scheme of things.

Pema Chödrön

Life is expressed in a perpetual sequence of changes.
The birth of the child is the death of the baby,
just as the birth of the adolescent is the death of the child.

Arnaud Desjardins

The trouble is that you think you have time.

Jack Kornfield

We must look at our life without sentimentality, exaggeration or idealism.

Does what we are choosing reflect what we most deeply value?

Jack Kornfield

*Modern civilization is largely devoted to the pursuit of the cult of delusion.
There is no general information about the nature of mind. It is hardly ever written about by
writers or intellectuals; modern philosophers do not speak of it directly; the majority of scientists deny
it could possibly be there at all. It plays no part in popular culture: no one sings about it,
no one talks about it in plays, and it's not on TV. We are actually educated into believing that
nothing is real beyond what we can perceive with our ordinary senses.*

Sogyal Rinpoche

Ignorance refers to a fundamental misperception of the true nature of the self and all phenomena.

The 14th Dalai Lama

There is nothing clever about not being happy.

Arnaud Desjardins

*The most important thing is the way we act from moment to moment
in our everyday life, just as it happens. To escape from the nightmare,
we must build an inner structure over which the mind has no hold,
and which spans all areas of our lives: intellectual, emotional, sexual.*

Arnaud Desjardins

What counts is not the enormity of the task, but the size of the courage.

Matthieu Ricard

Great spiritual traditions are used as means to ripen us,
to bring us face to face with our life, and to help us to see in a
new way by developing a stillness of mind and a strength of heart.

Jack Kornfield

Underneath our ordinary lives, underneath all the talking we do, all the moving we do,
all the thoughts in our minds, there's a fundamental groundlessness. It's there bubbling along all the time.
We experience it as restlessness and edginess. We experience it as fear. It motivates passion,
aggression, ignorance, jealousy, and pride, but we never get down to the essence of it.

Pema Chödrön

Feelings like disappointment, embarrassment, irritation, resentment, anger, jealousy, and fear, instead of being bad news, are actually very clear moments that teach us where it is that we're holding back.

Pema Chödrön

As we willingly enter each place of fear, each place of deficiency and insecurity in ourselves,
we will discover that its walls are made of untruths, of old images of ourselves,
of ancient fears, of false ideas of what is pure and what is not.

Jack Kornfield

*Suffering begins to dissolve when we can question
the belief or the hope that there's anywhere to hide.*

Pema Chödrön

What we're talking about is getting to know fear, becoming familiar with fear,
looking it right in the eye — not as a way to solve problems, but as a
complete undoing of old ways of seeing, hearing, smelling, tasting and thinking.
The truth is that when we really begin to do this, we're going to be continually humbled.

Pema Chödrön

We are awakened to the profound realization that
the true path to liberation is to let go of everything.

Jack Kornfield

*You cannot live sheltered forever without ever being exposed, and at the
same time be a spiritual adventurer. Be audacious. Be crazy in your own way,
with that madness in the eyes of man that is wisdom in the eyes of God.
Take risks, search and search again, search everywhere, in every way,
do not let a single opportunity or chance that life offers pass you by,
and do not be petty and mean, trying to drive a hard bargain.*

Arnaud Desjardins

We must especially learn the art of directing mindfulness into the closed areas of our life.

Jack Kornfield

It is right mindfulness and attention that allow us to change our behaviour.

Kalu Rinpoche

We must have the courage to face whatever is present.

Jack Kornfield

Usually we think that brave people have no fear.
The truth is that they are intimate with fear.

Pema Chödrön

Nothing goes right on the outside when nothing is going right on the inside.

Matthieu Ricard

You menace others with your deadly fangs
But in tormenting them, you are only torturing yourselves.

Milarepa

To diminish the suffering of pain, we need to make a crucial distinction between the pain of pain, and the pain we create by our thoughts about the pain. Fear, anger, guilt, loneliness and helplessness are all mental and emotional responses that can intensify pain.

Howard Cutler

31 May

Learning to live is learning to let go.

Sogyal Rinpoche

When the mind is full of memories and preoccupied by the future,
it misses the freshness of the present moment. In this way,
we fail to recognize the luminous simplicity of mind
that is always present behind the veils of thought.

Matthieu Ricard

We can always begin again.

Jack Kornfield

On days when the sky is grey, the sun has not disappeared forever.

Arnaud Desjardins

Things falling apart is a kind of testing and also a kind of healing.

Pema Chödrön

6 June

When there's a disappointment, I don't know if it's the end of the story.

But it may be just the beginning of a great adventure.

Pema Chödrön

When repeated difficulties do arise,
our first spiritual approach is to acknowledge what is present, naming,
softly saying 'sadness, sadness', or 'remembering, remembering', or whatever.

Jack Kornfield

Our hearts can grow strong at the broken places.

Quoted by Jack Kornfield

Every event, every situation in which you may find yourself has a positive value,
even the dramas, even the tragedies, even the thunderbolt from a calm sky.

Arnaud Desjardins

Thinking that we can find some lasting pleasure
and avoid pain is what in Buddhism is called samsara,
a hopeless cycle that goes round and round
endlessly and causes us to suffer greatly.

Pema Chödrön

If hate reigns supreme, it chains us to hell.

Great avarice opens the gulf of eternal hunger.

Dull ignorance makes us no better than animals.

Growing passion ties us to the world of men.

If jealousy takes root, it leads to the realm of warring gods.

Overbearing pride traps us in the land of the heavens.

These are the six fetters that chain us to samsara.

Milarepa

It seems that often when problems arise, our outlook becomes narrow.

The 14th Dalai Lama

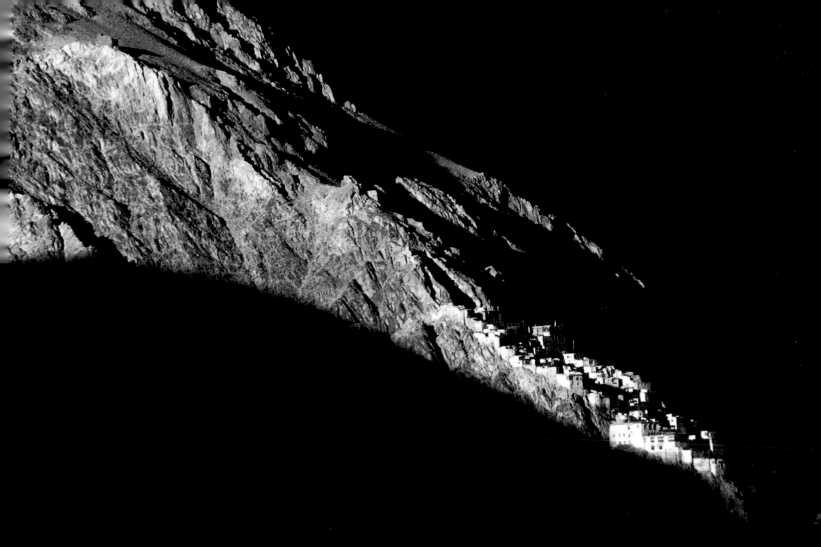

Enemies such as craving and hatred are without arms or legs.

They are neither courageous nor wise. How is it that they have enslaved me?

Shantideva

Invisible suffering is the latent suffering that is present in all that we are,
in the guise of ignorance, attachment to the self, and a false perception of reality.

Matthieu Ricard

It's painful to face how we harm others, and it takes a while.
It's a journey that happens because of our commitment to gentleness and honesty,
our commitment to staying awake, to being mindful.

Pema Chödrön

We continue to create suffering, waging war with good,
waging war with evil, waging war with what is too small,
waging war with what is too big, waging war with what is too short
or too long, or right or wrong, courageously carrying on the battle.

Achaan Chah

The near enemy of loving-kindness is attachment. At first, attachment may feel like love,
but as it grows it becomes more clearly the opposite, characterized by clinging, controlling, and fear.

The near enemy of compassion is pity, and this also separates us.
Pity feels sorry for that poor person over there as if he were somehow different from us.

The near enemy of sympathetic joy (the joy in the happiness of others) is comparison,
which looks to see if we have more than, the same as, or less than another.

The near enemy of equanimity is indifference. True equanimity is balance
in the midst of experience, whereas indifference is a withdrawal and not caring, based on fear.

Jack Kornfield

Gratitude leads to love. But not to demanding love, the love of a hunter for his prey. Do not confuse begging love with the generous love that leads to thankfulness.

Arnaud Desjardins

*Envy and jealousy stem from the fundamental inability
to rejoice at someone else's happiness or success.*

Matthieu Ricard

When we step out of the battle we see anew, with 'eyes unclouded by longing'.

Jack Kornfield

You should begin to build up confidence and joy in your own richness.
That richness is the essence of generosity. It is the sense of resourcefulness,
that you can deal with whatever is available around you and not feel poverty-stricken.

Chögyam Trungpa

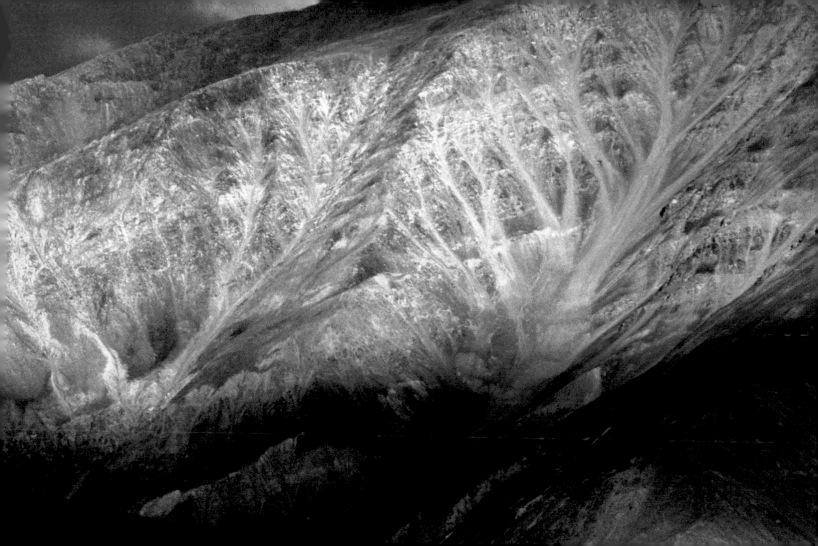

To taste the full spread of the joys of samsara, such as wealth and other pleasures,
is like tasting poisoned food, licking honey from a razor's edge;
in short it is a jewel on the head of a rattlesnake; one touch and you are annihilated.

Shabkar

The rich never have enough money, and the powerful never have enough power.

Let us reflect: the best way to satisfy all our desires and make all our plans come to fruition is to let them go.

Dilgo Khyentse Rinpoche

One interesting thing about greed is that although the underlying motive
is to seek satisfaction, the irony is that even after obtaining the object of your desire
you are still not satisfied. The true antidote of greed is contentment.

The 14th Dalai Lama

From possessiveness is born need
From non-attachment, satisfaction.

Kalu Rinpoche

Children, old people, vagabonds laugh easily and heartily: they have nothing to lose and hope for little. In renunciation lies a delicious taste of simplicity and deep peace.

Matthieu Ricard

Want what you have and don't want what you don't have.
Here you will find true fulfilment.

Quoted by Jack Kornfield

We want the world to allow the unconditional fulfilment of all our aspirations,

and since this does not happen, we fall prey to suffering.

Our search for happiness is more often founded on our illusions than on reality.

It is pointless to try to shape the world to fit our desires: we must transform our minds.

Matthieu Ricard

Without being aware of it, you take many things as being your identity:
your body, your race, your beliefs, your thoughts.

Jack Kornfield

True freedom means freeing oneself from the dictates of the ego and its accompanying emotions.

Matthieu Ricard

You are encouraged to say to your ego:
'You have created tremendous trouble for me,
and I don't like you. I'm going to destroy you.'

Chögyam Trungpa

All the harm, fear, and suffering in the world are caused by attachment to the self: why should I hold on to this great demon?

Shantideva

The essence of Buddhism: 'No self, no problem.'

Quoted by Jack Kornfield

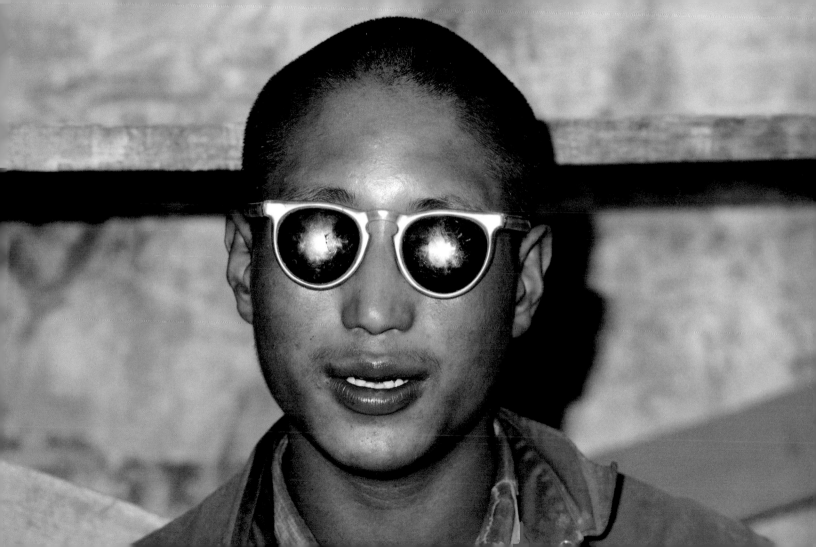

Even when we do receive good advice, it is easy to ignore it or misinterpret it. The places where we are stuck, those difficult layers of fear and attachment, the points of self-delusion and unworthiness we will encounter, are many. They come in everyone's practice, and the more educated and competent we believe ourselves to be, the slower the climb and the more foolhardy our falls.

Jack Kornfield

We can gradually drop our ideals of who we think we ought to be,

or who we think we want to be, or who we think other people think we want to be or ought to be.

Pema Chödrön

By breaking down our sense of self-importance,
all we lose is a parasite that has long infected our minds.
What we gain in return is freedom, openness of mind, spontaneity,
simplicity, altruism: all qualities inherent in happiness.

Matthieu Ricard

To take the one seat is to discover that we are unshakable.

Jack Kornfield

Humility does not mean believing oneself to be inferior, but to be freed from self-importance. It is a state of natural simplicity which is in harmony with our true nature and allows us to taste the freshness of the present moment.

Matthieu Ricard

Yes *and* **thank you** *are the opposites of selfishness.*
The ego can only be erased through happiness and gratitude.

Arnaud Desjardins

Ours is a society of denial that conditions us to
protect ourselves from any direct difficulty and discomfort.
We expend enormous energy denying our insecurity, fighting pain, death,
and loss, and hiding from the basic truths of the natural world and of our own nature.

Jack Kornfield

The best defence is built where your enemies are!
To be able to observe your vows and at the same time resist the
worldly temptations of an environment where so many circumstances
tend to awaken one's desires — is this not admirable, marvellous behaviour?

The 14th Dalai Lama

*In opening we can see how many times we have mistaken small identities
and fearful beliefs for our true nature, and how limiting this is.
We can touch with great compassion the pain from the contracted identities
that we and others have created in the world.*

Jack Kornfield

The key is changing our habits and, in particular, the habits of our mind.

Pema Chödrön

We really don't want to stay with the nakedness of our present experience.
It goes against the grain to stay present. There are the times when only gentleness
and a sense of humour can give us the strength to settle down.

Pema Chödrön

Our lives are lived in intense and anxious struggle,
in a swirl of speed and aggression, in competing, grasping, possessing and achieving,
forever burdening ourselves with extraneous activities and preoccupations.

Sogyal Rinpoche

Western laziness consists of cramming our lives with compulsive activity,
so that there is no time at all to confront the real issues.

Sogyal Rinpoche

Simplifying our lives does not mean sinking into idleness,
but on the contrary, getting rid of the most subtle aspect of laziness:
the one which makes us take on thousands of less important activities.

Matthieu Ricard

In a society that almost demands life at double time,
speed and addictions numb us to our own experience. In such a society
it is almost impossible to settle into our bodies or stay connected with our hearts,
let alone connect with one another or the earth where we live.

Jack Kornfield

Becoming immersed in these four pairs of opposites — pleasure and pain, loss and gain, fame and disgrace, and praise and blame — is what keeps us stuck in the pain of samsara.

Pema Chödrön

Try to reverse samsaric logic a little bit to see what happens.

And what usually happens is that you become a gentle person.

Chögyam Trungpa

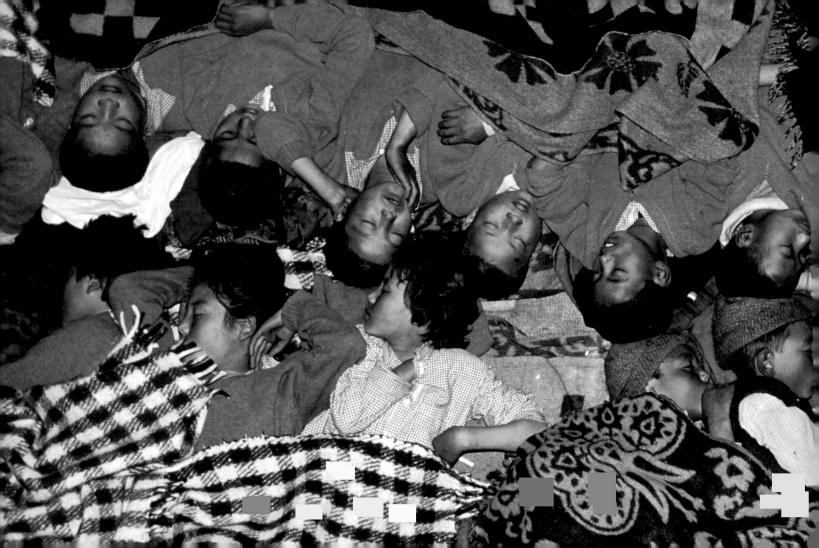

Would it not be a sane decision to renounce these mental poisons?
The time has finally come to stop these children's games, alternating between happiness and suffering.

Matthieu Ricard

31 July

*The art of happiness begins with developing an understanding
of what are the truest sources of happiness, and setting our priorities
in life based on the cultivation of those sources.*

Howard Cutler

Everything is based on our own uptightness. We could blame the organization;
we could blame the government; we could blame the food; we could blame the highways;
we could blame our own motorcars, our own clothes; we could blame an infinite variety of things.
But it is we who are not letting go, not developing enough warmth and sympathy —
which makes us problematic. So we cannot blame anybody.

Chögyam Trungpa

Renunciation contains an element of joy, struggle, enthusiasm and freedom:
it is the relief of finally being freed from dissatisfaction.

Matthieu Ricard

Everyone knows their own mind, but they do not know what it is to feel fulfilled. It is almost a mystical statement.

Arnaud Desjardins

Right now, at this very moment, we have a mind,

which is all the basic equipment we need to achieve complete happiness.

Howard Cutler

May I be born into a family neither rich nor poor

But into a modest home

So that I may easily renounce the place of my birth.

Shabkar

My bed is small, but I rest at ease,
My clothes are thin, but my body is warm,
My food is scarce, but I am nourished.

Milarepa

There are probably things in our lives from which we could unburden ourselves.

Matthieu Ricard

We must seek the true causes of happiness and satisfaction in ourselves.

The 14th Dalai Lama

Let us live simply in the freshness of the present moment,
in the clarity of pure awakened mind.

Matthieu Ricard

An adult is one who has lost the grace, the freshness, the innocence of the child,
who is no longer capable of feeling pure joy, who makes everything complicated,
who spreads suffering everywhere, who is afraid of being happy, and who,
because it is easier to bear, has gone back to sleep. The wise man is a happy child.

Arnaud Desjardins

On an evolutionary scale, the species that were most flexible,

most adaptable to environmental changes, survived and thrived.

A supple mind can help us reconcile the external changes going on all around us.

Howard Cutler

You can't stop the waves, but you can learn to surf.

Joseph Goldstein

A balanced and skilful approach to life, taking care to avoid extremes, becomes a very important factor in conducting one's everyday existence.

The 14th Dalai Lama

Life is movement.
The more life there is, the more flexibility there is.
The more fluid you are, the more you are alive.

Arnaud Desjardins

We have only now, only this single eternal moment
opening and unfolding before us, day and night.

Jack Kornfield

Let us reflect on what is truly of value in life,

what gives meaning to our lives, and set our priorities on the basis of that.

The 14th Dalai Lama

Confined in the dark, narrow cage of our own making which we take for the whole universe, very few of us can even begin to imagine another dimension of reality.

Sogyal Rinpoche

Daring to live means daring to die at any moment but also means daring to be born, crossing great stages of life in which the person we have been dies, and is replaced by another with a renewed vision of the world, and at the same time realizing that there will be many obstacles to overcome before we reach the final stage of Enlightenment.

Arnaud Desjardins

We each need to make our lion's roar — to persevere with unshakable courage
when faced with all manner of doubts and sorrows and fears — to declare our right to awaken.

Jack Kornfield

*Have the courage to throw yourself into life, take risks, weather blows,
knowing before you begin that you will be exposed to a series of opposites;
success and failure, happiness and unhappiness, praise and blame.*

Arnaud Desjardins

Mindful and creative, a child who has neither a past, nor examples to follow, nor value judgments, simply lives, speaks and plays in freedom.

Arnaud Desjardins

Saying yes, opening up, and loving:
these are the keys that will unlock the prison door.

Arnaud Desjardins

Generosity enacts the quality of non-greed; it is willingness to give, to share, to let go.
We are inspired to give because of loving feeling, and in the act of giving we feel more love.

Joseph Goldstein

The Buddha talked of morality as being the true beauty of a person.

It is the goodness that really shines on the inside of a person.

This is one of the greatest contributions we can give to the world,

for our non-harming offers the gift of safety and trust to all those around us.

Joseph Goldstein

Respect leads to caring — a quality of impeccability in what we do.
Respect and faith nourish each other and give birth to many skilful actions.
As we foster the quality of respect in our lives, we can also begin to see the world in a different light.
The tone of caring that arises from giving respect can transform how we interact with society.
We begin to explore the possibilities of service, of taking an active role in seeing
what needs doing and lending our energy to those endeavours. Compassion motivates us to act,
and wisdom ensures the means are effective.

Joseph Goldstein

Listening itself is an art. When we listen with a still and concentrated mind,
it's possible to actually be responsive to what the words are saying.
Sometimes deep insights come in a flash, unexpectedly.

Joseph Goldstein

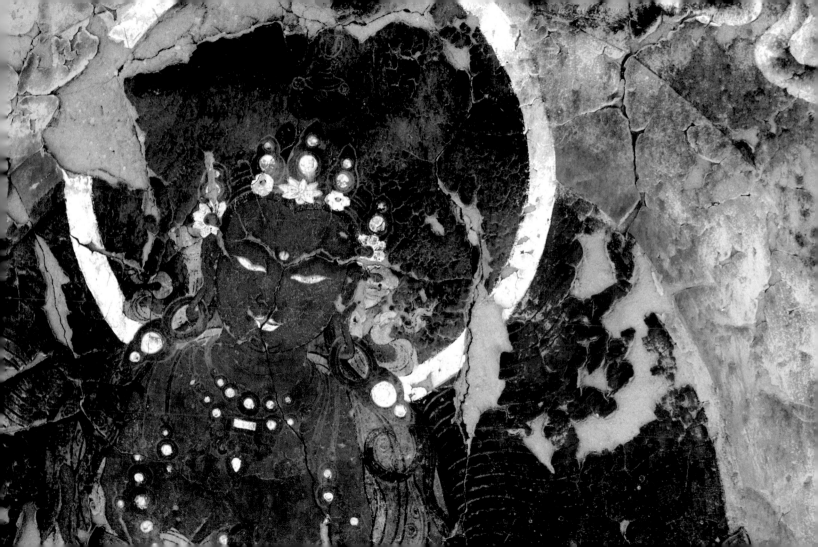

From concentration comes the birth of wisdom. Meditation begins with calming the mind and collecting the attention. In addition to the feelings of restfulness and peace, the state of concentration also becomes the basis for deepening insight and wisdom. We find ourselves opening to the world's suffering as well as to its great beauty.

Joseph Goldstein

Generosity, morality, respect, service, listening to the Dharma, and meditation —
these are actions for the good. Each one is a practice that can be cultivated and further refined,
becoming the causes for our own happiness and the happiness of others.
These acts for the good become our gift to the world.

Joseph Goldstein

If not here, where else could we bring alive compassion, justice, and liberation?

Jack Kornfield

Aggression is not essentially innate,
and violent behaviour is influenced by a variety of biological,
social, situational and environmental factors.

Howard Cutler

*Once we conclude that the basic nature of humanity is compassionate
rather than aggressive, our relationship to the world around us changes immediately.
Seeing others as basically compassionate instead of hostile and selfish helps us relax,
trust, live at ease. It makes us happier.*

Howard Cutler

Every conflict begins with thoughts of fear, animosity and aggression,
which pass through some people's minds and spread like wildfire.
The only antidote to these aberrations is to take on fully the suffering of others.

Matthieu Ricard

It is our mind, and that alone, that chains us or sets us free.

Dilgo Khyentse Rinpoche

Let the visions you experience pass through your consciousness
like clouds passing through an empty sky.

Jack Kornfield

When the mind is haughty, sarcastic, full of conceit and arrogance, ridiculing,

evasive and deceitful, when it is inclined to boast, or when it is contemptuous of others,

abusive and irritable, then remain still like a piece of wood.

Shantideva

Inordinate love of the body makes fear arise at the slightest danger:
so should one not abhor that body like a terrifying enemy? Should one not hate that self who,
from a desire to combat sickness, hunger and thirst, kills birds, fish, animals
and becomes an enemy of all living things? A self who, for love of gain or honour,
would even kill its own mother and father?

Shantideva

Most of us have spent our lives caught up in plans, expectations,

ambitions for the future, in regrets, guilt or shame about the past.

To come into the present is to stop the war.

Jack Kornfield

*All forms of hatred melt away, from the simple fact
of not liking someone to the revulsion felt towards murderers.*

Matthieu Ricard

It is the motivation behind an act that determines whether it is violent or non-violent.

Non-violent behaviour is a physical act or speech motivated by the wish to be useful or helpful.

The 14th Dalai Lama

A feeling of warmth creates a kind of openness.
You'll find that all human beings are just like you.

The 14th Dalai Lama

True compassion arises from a healthy sense of self,
from an awareness of who we are that honours our own capacities and fears,
our own feelings and integrity, along with those of others.

Jack Kornfield

*Bring your attention to the pain as if you were gently comforting a child,
holding it all in a loving and soothing attention.*

Jack Kornfield

Begin to recite inwardly the following phrases directed to yourself.

You begin with yourself because without loving yourself it is almost impossible to love others.

May I be filled with loving-kindness.

May I be well.

May I be peaceful and at ease.

May I be happy.

Jack Kornfield

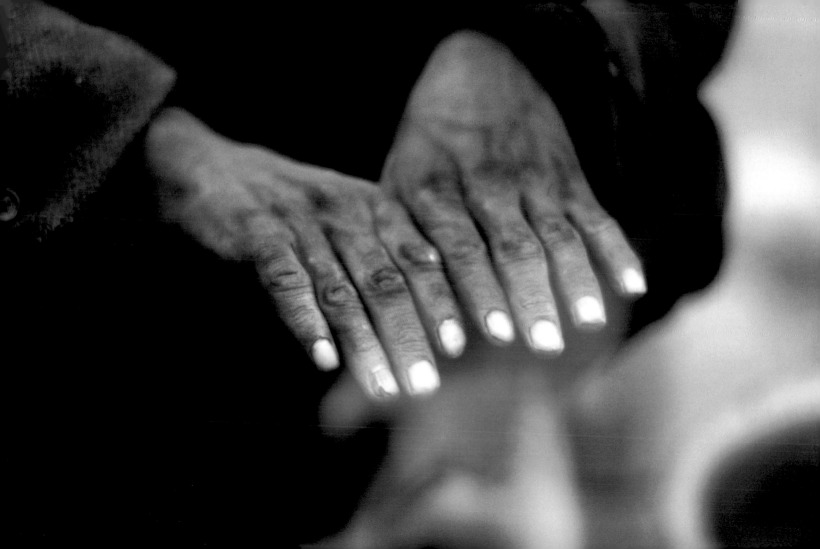

When you meditate, invite yourself to feel the self-esteem,
the dignity, and strong humility of the Buddha that you are.

Sogyal Rinpoche

If grief or anger arises, let there be grief or anger.

This is the Buddha in all forms, Sun Buddha, Moon Buddha, Happy Buddha, Sad Buddha.

It is the universe offering all things to awaken and open our heart.

Jack Kornfield

Compassion for ourselves gives rise to the power to transform resentment into forgiveness, hatred into friendliness, and fear into respect for all beings.

Jack Kornfield

Our companion or partner is perfect,
but we may wish that they were still as beautiful as they once were.
This only proves that we have forgotten the imminence of death.

Dilgo Khyentse Rinpoche

From the moment that a man and a woman are united by their karma,

they should spend every moment in search of harmony.

Dilgo Khyentse Rinpoche

The act of acceptance, of acknowledging that change is a natural part of our interaction with others, can play a vital role in our relationships. These transitional periods can become pivotal points when true love can begin to mature and flower. We are now in a position to truly begin to know the other. To see the other as a separate individual, with faults and weaknesses perhaps, but a human being like ourselves. It is only at this point that we can make a genuine commitment, a commitment to the growth of another human being — an act of true love.

Howard Cutler

Our capacity for intimacy is built on deep respect,
a presence that allows what is true to express itself,
to be discovered. Intimacy can arise in any moment;
it is an act of surrender, a gift that excludes nothing.

Jack Kornfield

Peace must develop on mutual trust.

The 14th Dalai Lama

This is not a matter of changing anything but of not grasping anything,
and of opening our eyes and our heart.

Jack Kornfield

The reality is that nobody is one hundred per cent bad.
They must have some good qualities if you search hard enough.
So, the tendency to see someone as completely negative is due to
your own perception based on your own mental projection,
rather than the true nature of that individual.

The 14th Dalai Lama

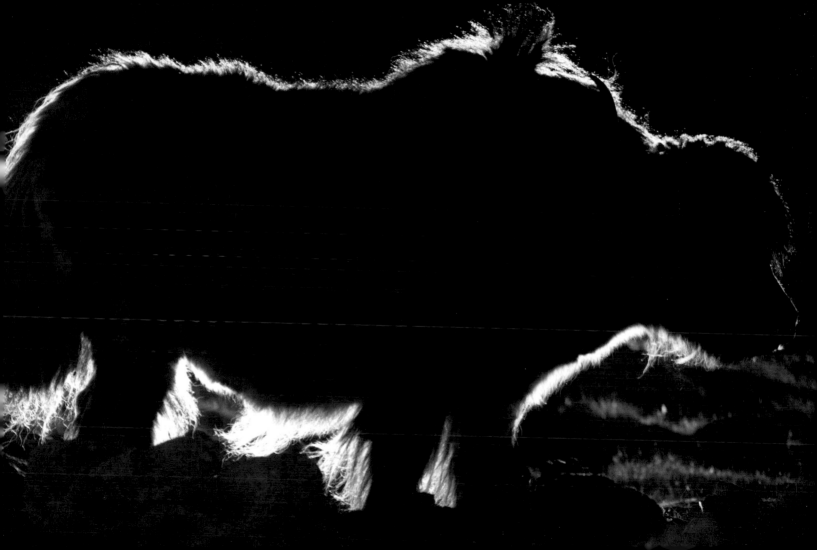

All those who are unhappy in the world are so as a result of their desire for their own happiness.

All those who are happy in the world are so as a result of their desire for the happiness of others.

Shantideva

In the valley, we have some friends whom we love, some enemies whom we hate,
and all the others whom we do not know. This perception of people is distorted and limited,
and produces nothing but attachment and aggression.

Dilgo Khyentse Rinpoche

Limbs are cherished because they are parts of the body:

why then are other people not cherished because they are parts of humanity?

Shantideva

We must understand each other and work in harmony with one another,
because it is our responsibility to develop in human beings their natural disposition for peace.

The 14th Dalai Lama

We can bring a heart of understanding and compassion to a world that needs it so much.

Jack Kornfield

When happiness is equally dear to others and myself,
then what is so special about me that I strive after happiness for myself alone?
When fear and suffering are equally abhorrent to others and myself,
then what is so special about me that I protect myself but not others?

Shantideva

9 October

Each act of generosity is a recognition of our interdependence,
an expression of our Buddha nature.

Jack Kornfield

If we think about the vast majority of human problems,
both on a personal and on a worldwide scale, it seems that they stem from
an inability to feel sincerely involved with others, and to put ourselves in their place.
Violence is inconceivable if everyone is genuinely concerned with the happiness of others.

Matthieu Ricard

Sending and taking is regarded as a natural course of exchange; it just takes place.

Chögyam Trungpa

I look at every human being from a more positive angle; I try to look for their positive aspects. This attitude immediately creates a feeling of affinity, a kind of connectedness.

The 14th Dalai Lama

Those who wish to protect themselves and others swiftly
Should practise the great secret: exchanging oneself for others.

Shantideva

We do not realize often enough that we are dependent on one another;
at the simplest material level, we are all interdependent for our daily needs,
and in this way we owe a debt to all beings.

Kalu Rinpoche

We can give something to others.

We don't always have to receive something first in order to give something away.

Chögyam Trungpa

Our children are our meditation.

Jack Kornfield

The family is the most fundamental unit of society.

The 14th Dalai Lama

One family can influence another, then another, then ten,
one hundred, one thousand more, and the whole of society will benefit.

The 14th Dalai Lama

True love for our neighbour will be translated into courage and strength.
The more we develop love for others, the more confidence we will have in ourselves.

The 14th Dalai Lama

I began to think about how many people were involved in the making of my shirt.
I started by imagining the farmer who grew the cotton. Next, the hundreds
or even thousands of people involved in the manufacturing of the tractor.
And all the designers of the tractor. Then, of course the people who processed the cotton,
the people who wove the cloth, and the people who cut, dyed and sewed that cloth.
The cargo workers and the truck drivers who delivered the shirt to the store
and the sales person who sold the shirt to me. It occurred to me that
virtually every aspect of my life came about as the results of others' efforts.

Howard Cutler

*Without the rigidity of concepts, the world becomes transparent and illuminated,
as though lit from within. With this understanding, the interconnectedness of all that lives becomes very clear.
We see that nothing is stagnant and nothing is fully separate, that who we are, what we are, is intimately woven
into the nature of life itself. Out of this sense of connection, love and compassion arise.*

Sharon Salzberg

The laws that govern wise relationships in politics, marriage, or business are the same as in inner life. Each of these areas requires a capacity for commitment and constancy, for taking the one seat.

Jack Kornfield

It is important to understand how much your own happiness is linked to that of others.
There is no individual happiness totally independent of others.

The 14th Dalai Lama

Love, love, take the first step. Everything depends on love.
Even professional success means feeling that life loves you,
that your managers, bosses and colleagues are not enemies.

Arnaud Desjardins

Notions such as 'my country', 'your country, 'my religion', 'your religion' have become minor.

We must, on the contrary, insist on the fact that the other person is as worthy as we are.

This is humanity! This is why we must re-examine our educational system.

The 14th Dalai Lama

The wars between peoples are a reflection of our own inner conflict and fear.

Jack Kornfield

Hatred and malice are the greatest dangers to peace and happiness.
In order to prevent hatred and anger from taking root in ourselves,
we must first of all avoid discontent, for it is the root of hatred and malice.
Once hatred is expressed with all its strength and power,
it is very difficult to find an antidote to it.

The 14th Dalai Lama

We do not become angry with the stick that hits us,
but with the one who wields the stick.
But the one who wields the stick is impelled by hatred,
so what we should truly hate is hatred itself.

Shantideva

When everyone practises self-control through internal discipline,
there is no crime despite the absence of policemen in the world outside.
This demonstrates the importance of self-discipline.

The 14th Dalai Lama

*Compassion can be roughly defined in terms of a state of mind
that is non-violent, non-harming and non-aggressive. It is a mental attitude based on
the wish for others to be free of their suffering and is associated with a sense
of commitment, responsibility and respect towards others.
In discussing the definition of compassion, the Tibetan word* tse-wa,
*there is also a sense to the word of its being a state of mind that can include a wish
for good things for oneself. In developing compassion, perhaps one could begin with
the wish that oneself be free of suffering, and then take that natural feeling towards oneself
and cultivate it, enhance it, and extend it out to include and embrace others.*

The 14th Dalai Lama

What is an enemy? An enemy is someone who tries to hurt us,
our body, our belongings, our family, and our friends — in short,
anything that brings us happiness. The true enemy, therefore, is malice.

The 14th Dalai Lama

Something must be done about the trafficking of arms because the situation has become both terrifying and irresponsible. Reigns of terror are imposed by weapons.
For as long as there are such weapons, a disaster is still possible because we are constantly at the mercy of a handful of irresponsible people. As for me, I still advocate what I call inner disarmament through the reduction of hatred and the promotion of compassion.

The 14th Dalai Lama

I think that there is a very close connection between humility and patience. Humility involves having the capacity to take a more confrontational stance, having the capacity to retaliate if you wish, yet deliberately deciding not to do so. That is what I would call genuine humility. I think that true tolerance or patience has a component or element of self-discipline and restraint — the realization that you could have acted otherwise, you could have adopted a more aggressive approach, but decided not to do so.

The 14th Dalai Lama

I believe that to have world peace we must first have inner peace.

Those who are naturally serene, at peace with themselves, will be open towards others.

I think this is where the very foundation of universal peace lies.

The 14th Dalai Lama

All human beings have in common the desire
to avoid suffering and to know happiness.

The 14th Dalai Lama

The law commands us to do what we would do naturally if we only had love.

The Way consists of finding that love, which then becomes the law.

Arnaud Desjardins

The primary method to overcome social afflictions
is self-discipline in personal life,
through which one attempts to master self-control;
it is very difficult to impose discipline from the outside.

The 14th Dalai Lama

*You can feel compassion regardless of whether
you view the other person as a friend or an enemy.
It is based on the other's fundamental rights
rather than your own mental projection.*

The 14th Dalai Lama

There is a strong link between happiness and tolerance,
in so far as less prejudice means greater happiness.
The greater the social awareness and charitable involvement,
the greater is the happiness of the citizens.

Matthieu Ricard

We are all equal now, members of one and the same family,
and the affairs of the entire world are now internal affairs.

The 14th Dalai Lama

In one sense one could define compassion as the feeling of unbearableness
at the sight of other people's suffering, other sentient beings' suffering.
True compassion implies the wish to put an end to others' suffering
and a sense of responsibility for those who suffer.

The 14th Dalai Lama

Since patience or tolerance comes from an ability to remain firm and steadfast and not be overwhelmed by the adverse situations or conditions that one faces, one should not see tolerance or patience as a kind of weakness, or giving in, but rather as a sign of strength, coming from a deep ability to remain firm.

The 14th Dalai Lama

Courage to the fearful, freedom to the enslaved,
strength to the weak, mutual affection to all sentient beings.

Shantideva

When you speak of adopting a wider perspective,
this includes working cooperatively with other people.

The 14th Dalai Lama

The Buddha discovered what he called the Middle Way,
a way not based on an aversion to the world, nor on attachment, but a way
based on inclusion and compassion. The Middle Way rests at the centre
of all things, the one great seat in the centre of the world.

Jack Kornfield

The wisdom of the heart can be found in any circumstance, on any planet,
round or square. It arises not through knowledge or images of perfection,
or by comparison and judgment, but by seeing with the eyes of wisdom and the
heart of loving attention, by touching with compassion all that exists in our world.

Jack Kornfield

*Every morning, our first thought should be
a wish to devote the day to the good of all living beings.*

Dilgo Khyentse Rinpoche

*May no sentient being be unhappy, malicious, ill,
neglected, or despised; and may no one be despondent.*

Shantideva

Compassion is the heart's response to sorrow.
We share in the beauty of life and in the ocean of tears.
The sorrow of life is part of each of our hearts and part of what
connects us with one another. It brings with it tenderness, mercy,
and an all-embracing kindness that can touch every being.

Jack Kornfield

Wisdom and compassion should become the dominating influences that guide our thoughts, our words, and our actions.

Matthieu Ricard

An enemy is a rare thing.

The 14th Dalai Lama

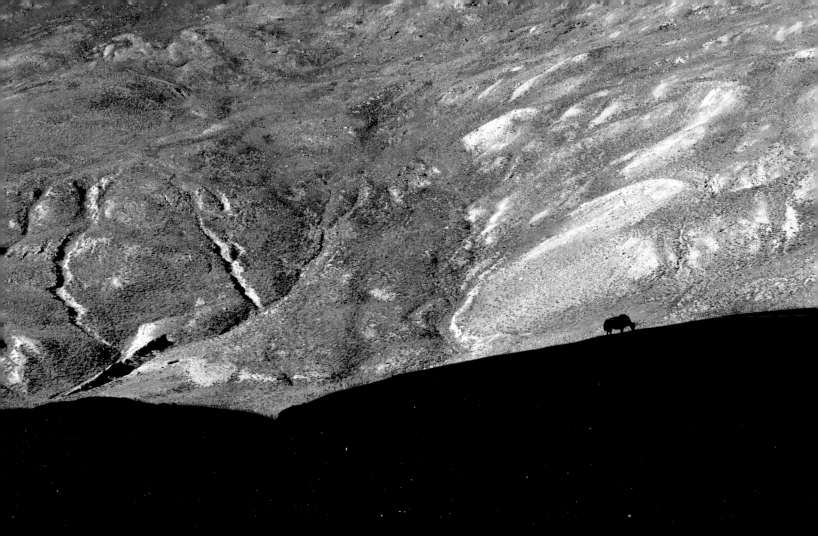

In the past all of life was based on trees. Their flowers gave us nourishment,
their leaves and fibres clothed us and provided us with shelter.
We took refuge in their branches for protection from wild animals.
We used wood for heat, and for canes to bear our weight when we grew old,
and to make weapons to defend ourselves. We were very close to trees.
Today, surrounded by sophisticated machinery and high-performance computers
in our ultra-modern offices, it is easy to forget our ties with nature.

The 14th Dalai Lama

The only way to reach the supernatural is through nature.

Arnaud Desjardins

There is beauty to be found in the changing of the earth's seasons,
and an inner grace in honouring the cycles of life.

Jack Kornfield

Where can fish and animals be taken where they could not be killed?

The renunciation of doing harm is the perfection of discipline.

Shantideva

According to Buddhism, the life of all beings — human, animal,
or otherwise — is precious, and all have the same right to happiness.
It is certain that birds, wild animals — all the creatures inhabiting our planet —
are our companions. They are a part of our world, we share it with them.

The 14th Dalai Lama

Just like space
And the great elements such as earth,
May I always support the life
Of all the boundless creatures.
And until they pass away from pain,
May I also be the source of life
For all the realms of varied beings
That reach unto the ends of space.

Shantideva

All of spiritual practice is a matter of relationship:
to ourselves, to others, to life's situations.

Jack Kornfield

With wise understanding we can live in harmony

with our life, with the universal law.

Jack Kornfield

12 December

This paper is empty of an independent self. Empty, in this sense,
means that the paper is full of everything, the entire cosmos.
The presence of this tiny sheet of paper proves the presence of the whole cosmos.

Thich Nhat Hanh

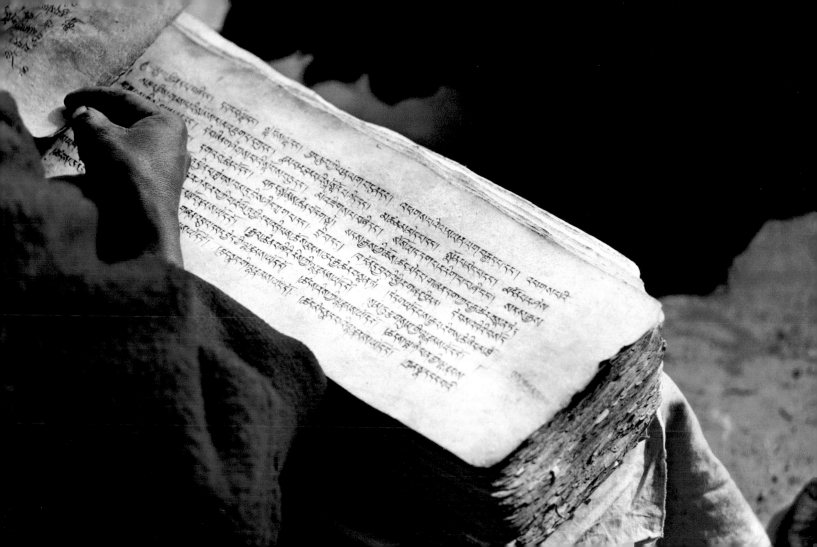

The forces which move the cosmos are no different
from those which move the human soul.

Lama Anagarika Govinda

*True spirituality is to be aware that if we are interdependent
with everything and everyone else, even our smallest, least significant thought,
word, and action have real consequences throughout the universe.*

Sogyal Rinpoche

Theism is a deep-seated conviction that there is some hand to hold.

Pema Chödrön

By feeling gratitude towards life, I move towards light, wholeness, universal energy, love. I move beyond the bounds of my own life and discover that I am an expression or form of universal life, of divine energy.

Arnaud Desjardins

18 December

Every step is an important advance towards deep satisfaction and fulfilment. The spiritual journey is like travelling from valley to valley: crossing each mountain pass reveals a more magnificent landscape than the one before.

Matthieu Ricard

Only in the reality of the present can we love, can we awaken,
can we find peace and understanding and connection with ourselves and the world.

Jack Kornfield

All that is visible clings to the invisible,
the audible to the inaudible,
the tangible to the intangible,
Perhaps the thinkable to the unthinkable.

Lama Anagarika Govinda

You will not reach love without immense gratitude in your heart.

Arnaud Desjardins

Everything that appears is singing one song, which is the song of emptiness and fullness.

We experience the world of phenomena and consciousness, of light and dark,

playing themselves out in a dance without separation.

Jack Kornfield

Reality, enlightenment or the divine must shine
through every moment or it is not genuine.

Jack Kornfield

Just as there is no point of darkness in the sun,
For the yogi, the universe and sentient beings are all deities,
And he is fulfilled.

Shabkar

The further you progress,
the more you will perceive that the universe is divine.

Arnaud Desjardins

Birds that live on a golden mountain reflect the colour of the gold.

Tibetan proverb

*The pure nature of mind — emptiness, lucidity
and intelligence without limit — has always been inside us.*

Kalu Rinpoche

Remember these teachings, remember the clear light,
the pure bright shining white light of your own nature. It is deathless.

The Tibetan Book of the Dead

We are already *wisdom.*

Arnaud Desjardins

About the Authors

Olivier and Danielle Föllmi, together with their four Tibetan children, divide their lives between the Alps and the Himalayas. Olivier has been photographing the Himalayas for twenty-five years, and his images have been seen all over the world and have won prizes including the World Press Award. An emergency doctor and anaesthetist, Danielle has set up health and nutrition programmes in Tibetan schools. They are the founders of HOPE, an educational charity for the Himalayas. They have produced many books, including *Buddhist Himalayas: People, Faith and Nature* (with Matthieu Ricard), and are keen to raise international awareness of Tibetan cultural heritage.

Born in Germany in 1898, **Lama Anagarika Govinda** was the founder of the Buddhist order Arya Maitreya Mandala. His keen interest in Pali Buddhism and monastic life led him to Sri Lanka and Burma. He also lived for several years in Tibet, before settling in Almora in India where he became a teacher and held exhibitions of his paintings. He travelled to the US and Canada in 1971, and to Europe in 1972, and became a campaigner for peace between East and West. His books include *The Foundations of Tibetan Mysticism*. He died in 1986.

Buddha Shakyamuni was born in Lumbini, in the modern kingdom of Nepal, in the sixth century BC, into the Shakya clan, part of the *ksatriya* (ruling or warrior) caste. Up to the age of 29, he lived in a palace, sheltered from the outside world, until he was suddenly made aware of the realities of life: poverty, sickness, old age and death. Overwhelmed, he became an ascetic in 531 BC. After subjecting himself to great physical deprivation, he realized that only the 'Middle Way', the avoidance of extremes, would allow him to reach Enlightenment. Buddhist literature contains many stories about his life.

The 11th incarnation of the Tulku Trungpa lineage, **Chögyam Trungpa** (1939–87) was the most well-known Tibetan Buddhist master resident in the US, and is recognized as one of the outstanding figures of the new generation of Tibetan teachers. He became a novice monk at the age of 8 and began the traditional monastic disciplines of intensive practice and study. In 1958, at the age of 18, he became a fully ordained monk. He had a talent for presenting the traditional Vajrayana teachings in a modern way to a wide audience. He also founded the Naropa Institute and the Shambhala learning programme. His published works include *Training the Mind and Cultivating Loving-Kindness*.

His Holiness the 14th Dalai Lama Tenzin Gyatso, spiritual and temporal leader of the Tibetan people, was born on 6 July 1935 in Taktser, a small village in north-eastern Tibet, to a peasant family. At the age of two,

His Holiness was recognized as the reincarnation of his predecessor, the 13th Dalai Lama, and of the Buddha of Compassion, Avalokitesvara. His enthronement took place on 22 February 1940 in Lhasa. He left Tibet for India after the Chinese occupation. Since his exile to Dharamsala, he has continued to campaign for a diplomatic solution to the Tibetan question, work for which he was awarded the Nobel Prize for Peace in 1989.

Born in 1925, **Arnaud Desjardins** was brought up in a Christian Protestant background. After spending time at Himalayan monasteries from 1964 to 1967, he made a series of films about spiritual teachers from different Asian traditions. He used these to teach the West about the living spiritual traditions of the East, and also to deepen his own spiritual quest. He spent years studying with his teacher Swami Prajnanpad until the latter's death in 1974, when Desjardins returned to central France and began to pass on the teachings he had received. His books have been translated and published all over the world.

Greatly respected in Tibet and throughout the world, **Dilgo Khyentse Rinpoche** (1910–91) was one of the greatest poets, scholars, philosophers and meditation masters of all 20th-century Tibetan Buddhist traditions. He received teachings and transmissions from over fifty lamas and engaged in solitary practice for 22 years. Afterwards, he worked tirelessly to pass on these teachings, both in India and the Himalayan region and in the West and south-east Asia.

Dudjom Rinpoche (1904–88) was one of the three incarnations of Dudjom Lingpa. He was exiled from Tibet and became the leader of the Nyingmapa school of Tibetan Buddhism. He was a poet, an artist, a musician and a sculptor, as well as the author of several books.

Co-founder and guiding teacher of the Insight Meditation Society (IMS), **Joseph Goldstein** has been teaching *vipassana* meditation since 1974. He first grew interested in Buddhism in Thailand in 1965, and he has studied and practised with eminent teachers from Burma, India and Tibet. In 1989 he helped to establish the Barre Center for Buddhist Studies. He is currently developing the Forest Refuge, a centre for long-term meditation practice. His books include *One Dharma: The Emerging Western Buddhism*.

Kalu Rinpoche (1904–89) was one of the greatest of contemporary spiritual teachers, respected by all Buddhist traditions. He began his training at Palpung Monastery at the age of 13, and went on to spend 25 years living as a hermit in the Kham mountains. He spent some twenty years teaching in the West, displaying the highest level of wisdom and compassion, the very essence of the Buddha's teachings.

Jack Kornfield is not only a Buddhist monk but also a clinical psychologist, psychotherapist, author and meditation teacher. After living as a monk in south-east Asia and India, he returned to the United States in 1972, where he co-founded the Insight Meditation Society (IMS) with Sharon Salzberg and Joseph Goldstein. He is also the founding teacher of the Spirit Rock Center, north of San Francisco, California, where he teaches *vipassana* meditation. His many books include *A Path With Heart*.

A semi-legendary Tibetan ascetic from the 11th century, Milarepa (1040–1123) was the disciple of Marpa, known as the Translator, and the founder of a school of mysticism which eventually became Tibetan Buddhism. Considered to be a symbol of Tibet, Milarepa is also the poet, ascetic and spiritual teacher incarnate.

A Tibetan teacher of the Nyingmapa school, Patrul Rinpoche was born into a nomadic family in Kham in the 19th century. Recognized as the incarnation of Shantideva, he followed the teachings of Jigme Lingpa and Gyalse Shenpen Thaye. His written works and commentaries include *The Words of My Perfect Teacher*.

Born in the US in 1936, Pema Chödrön has been a Buddhist nun since 1974. She is one of the principal disciples of the Tibetan master Chögyam Trungpa, and has been the director of Gampo Abbey in Canada since 1986. Her books include *Start Where You Are: A Guide to Compassionate Living* and *When Things Fall Apart: Heart Advice for Difficult Times*.

On his first trip to India in 1967, Matthieu Ricard met some remarkable Tibetan spiritual masters. After finishing his thesis in cellular genetics in 1972, he settled in the Himalayas where he became a monk, sharing in the teachings of Dilgo Khyentse Rinpoche. He currently lives in the Shechen Monastery in Nepal. He is a prolific photographer, writer and translator, as well as the French interpreter for the Dalai Lama. His books include *The Quantum and the Lotus* (with Trinh Xuan Thanh) and *Buddhist Himalayas: People, Faith and Nature* (with Danielle and Oliver Föllmi).

Co-founder of the Insight Meditation Society (IMS) and the Barre Center for Buddhist Studies, Sharon Salzberg has practised Buddhist meditation since 1971 and has taught worldwide since 1974, teaching both intensive awareness practice (*vipassana*) and the cultivation of loving-kindness and compassion. She is the author of *Faith: Trusting your Own Deepest Experience*, *Lovingkindness* and *A Heart as Wide as the World*.

The Tibetan hermit Shabkar (1781–1851) is revered by the Tibetan people for his holiness and simplicity, his ability to move people as well as make them laugh, and the depth of his spirituality, expressed in a style that is accessible to all. His book *The Life of Shabkar* recounts his travels in a prose style, intercut with poetic songs. His story illustrates Buddhist teachings on the meaning of life, death, and the possibility of an end to suffering.

An Indian saint of the 9th century, Shantideva shaped Buddhist literature with his spiritual understanding and genius. The writings of this Mahayana author are considered key texts in the Bodhisattva and Middle Way traditions, and have been closely studied for centuries. His beautiful poem *The Way of the Bodhisattva* still provides inspiration to thousands of readers.

Born in Kham in eastern Tibet, **Sogyal Rinpoche** was recognized as the incarnation of Lerab Lingpa Tertön Sogyal, a teacher to the 13th Dalai Lama. He studied with masters including Jamyang Khyentse, Dudjom Rinpoche and Dilgo Khyentse Rinpoche. As a translator and teacher, he travelled to many countries, observing the realities of people's lives and adapting his teachings to make them relevant to modern men and women. His book *The Tibetan Book of Living and Dying* has sold more than a million and a half copies in 26 languages. In 1992, he founded the Spiritual Care Program, which aims to bring the wisdom and compassion of his teachings to professional and trained volunteer caregivers.

Glossary of Buddhist Terms

Buddha-nature: not an 'entity' but the ultimate nature of pure consciousness, totally free from the veils of ignorance. Each being has the potential to reach a state of perfect knowledge of the nature of mind. In a sense, it is Buddhism's concept of the 'original goodness' in all beings.

Compassion: the desire to liberate all living beings from suffering and the causes of suffering (negative actions and ignorance). It is the complement of love (the wish for all beings to know happiness and the causes of happiness), of altruistic joy (rejoicing in the qualities of another) and of equanimity, which extends these feelings to all beings without distinction, friends, strangers and foes alike.

Dharma: a word of many meanings. At its broadest, it signifies everything that can be known. Most often, it denotes the totality of the teachings of the Buddhas and great teachers. There are two aspects to this: the dharma of the scriptures, which underpins these teachings, and the dharma of realization, which is the outcome of spiritual practice.

Enlightenment: synonymous with the condition of being a Buddha, Enlightenment is the ultimate accomplishment of spiritual growth, supreme inner knowledge, allied to infinite compassion. Perfect understanding of both relative existence (the way things appear to us) and of ultimate existence (their true nature) of the mind and of the world of phenomena. This knowledge is the basic antidote to ignorance and therefore to suffering.

Ignorance: an erroneous way of perceiving beings and things, attributing them with real, independent, solid and intrinsic existence.

Impermanence: there are two kinds, gross and subtle. Gross impermanence refers to visible changes. Subtle impermanence is the fact that nothing remains the same for more than the shortest conceivable moment of time.

Karma: a Sanskrit word meaning 'action', usually translated as 'causality of actions'. The Buddha taught that the destinies of beings, along with their joy, their suffering and their perception of the universe, are not due to either chance or the will of an all-powerful entity but are the outcome of their past actions, words and thoughts. Similarly, their future is determined by the positive or negative quality of their present actions. Collective karma defines our general perception of the world, while individual karma determines our personal experiences.

Meditation: process of familiarizing oneself with a new perception of things. Analytical meditation can take as its subject something on which to reflect (the notion of impermanence, for example) or a quality one wishes to develop (such as love or compassion). Contemplative meditation allows us to recognize the ultimate nature of mind and to remain in that nature, beyond conceptual thought.

Middle Way (Madhyamika): the highest philosophy of Buddhism, so-called because it avoids the two extremes of negation and affirmation of the reality of phenomena.

Mind: for Buddhism, mind, in its ordinary form, is characterized by illusion. A succession of instants of consciousness gives it the illusion of continuity. In its absolute form, mind is defined by three characteristics: emptiness, clarity and spontaneous compassion.

Samsara: the cycle of existence, marked by suffering and the frustration engendered by ignorance and the afflictive emotions it causes. It is only by knowing emptiness and thus dispelling all negative emotions that one may recognize the nature of mind and free oneself from samsara.

Suffering: the first of the Four Noble Truths, which are: 1) the truth of suffering, which we need to recognize as omnipresent in the cycle of existences; 2) the truth of the causes of suffering – the negative emotions we need to eliminate; 3) the truth of the Path of spiritual development that we must travel in order to achieve liberation; and 4) the truth of the end of suffering, resulting from spiritual training, or Enlightenment.

Wisdoms (Five): five aspects of Enlightenment: equalizing wisdom, mirror-like wisdom, discriminating wisdom, all-accomplishing wisdom, and wisdom of ultimate reality. These five wisdoms can only be actualized after the two veils which prevent Enlightenment have been dispersed: the veil of emotions that cloud perception and the veil masking knowledge of the ultimate nature of phenomena.

Sources of Quotations

Lama Anagarika Govinda, Published in *Les Fondements de la mystique tibétaine*. © 1960 Editions Albin Michel, Paris: 2 March; 13 and 20 December.

Chödrön, Pema, From *When Things Fall Apart: Heart Advice for Difficult Times*. © 1997 by Pema Chödrön. Reprinted by arrangement with Shambhala Publications, Inc., Boston, www.shambhala.com, and HarperCollins Ltd, London: 10 and 24 January; 17–18 and 26 February; 21 and 28 March; 9 and 30 April; 14, 15, 17, 18 and 26–27 May; 5, 6, 11 and 16–17 June; 10, 20, 21–22 and 27 July; 15–16 December.

Chödrön, Pema, From *Start Where You Are: A Guide to Compassionate Living*. © 1994 by Pema Chödrön. Reprinted by arrangement with Shambhala Publications, Inc., Boston, www.shambhala.com, and HarperCollins Ltd, London: 9 November.

Chögyam Trungpa, From *Training the Mind and Cultivating Lovingkindness*. © 1993 by Diana J. Mukpo. Reprinted by arrangement with Shambhala Publications, Inc., Boston, www.shambhala.com: 23–24 June; 5 and 28–29 July; 1 August; 11 and 16 October.

His Holiness the 14th Dalai Lama, From *Beyond Dogma: Dialogues and Discourses*, published by North Atlantic Books, Berkeley, CA. © 1996 North Atlantic Books. Reprinted by permission of the publisher: 12, 14, 15 and 16 February; 15 and 31 March–1 April; 17 July; 9 August; 14 September; 5, 20–21, 25, 27–28, 30 and 31 October; 2, 5, 6, 10–11, 14, 16 and 19 November; 3 and 7 December.

His Holiness the 14th Dalai Lama, Published in *Conseils du cœur*. © 2001 Presses de la Renaissance, Paris: 18 and 19 October.

His Holiness the 14th Dalai Lama, and Howard C. Cutler, From *The Art of Happiness: A Handbook for Living*. © 1999 by His Holiness the Dalai Lama and Howard C. Cutler. Reprinted by permission of Hodder & Stoughton Ltd, London: 6–7 and 13–14 January; 13 February; 1, 16 and 22 March; 20 and 27 April; 4, 8 and 30 May; 13 and 27 June; 31 July; 4–5, 13, 15 and 18–19 August; 4, 5, 15, 26 and 28 September; 1, 12 and 22 October; 3–4, 8, 12, 15, 20, 21 and 23 November; 1–2 December.

Desjardins, Arnaud, Published in *L'Audace de vivre*. © 1989 Editions de La Table Ronde, Paris: 26 January; 27 February; 1, 9, 10 and 21 May; 4, 9–10 and 20 June; 14–15 July; 3, 11–12, 16, 21, 23, 24 and 25–26 August; 26 October; 13 November; 4, 17, 21, 26 and 31 December.

Dilgo Khyentse Rinpoche, Published in *Les Cent conseils de Padampa Sangyé*. © 2000 Editions Padmakara, Saint-Léon-sur-Vézère: 3, 16, 17, 23 and 27–28 January; 8, 10–11, 12 and 14 March; 3, 6, 7–8, 18 and 23 April; 26 June; 7, 24 and 25 September; 3 October; 7 and 27 November.

Goldstein, Joseph, From *One Dharma. The Emerging Western Buddhism*. © 2002 by Insight Meditation Society. Reprinted by permission of HarperCollins Publishers Inc.: 6 March; 14, 27, 28, 29, 30 and 31 August; 1–2 September.

Kalu Rinpoche, Published in *La Voie du Bouddha selon la tradition tibétaine*, © 1993 Editions du Seuil, Paris: 4, 9, 12, 18 and 30 January; 3–4 and 20 February; 9, 24–25, 26 and 27 March; 16 and 26 April; 24 May; 28 June; 15 October; 28 December.

Kornfield, Jack, From *A Path with Heart: A Guide Through the Perils and Promises of Spiritual Life*. © 1993 by Jack Kornfield. Used by permission of Bantam Books, a division of Random House, Inc., New York: 11, 19 and 31 January; 1, 2, 5, 6, 7, 8, 9, 10, 19 and 22 February; 3–4, 5, 20 and 23 March; 4 and 21–22 April; 2, 3, 12–13, 16, 19–20, 22, 23 and 25 May; 2–3, 7, 8, 18, 19, 22 and 30 June; 3, 7–8, 9, 12, 16, 18, 19 and 26 July; 17, 18, 19, 21, 22–23, 27 and 29–30 September; 6–7, 9, 17, 24 and 29 October; 24–25, 26 and 29 November; 5, 10, 11, 12, 19, 22–23 and 24 December; page 11.

Milarepa, *The Hundred Thousand Songs of Milarepa*: 19 March; 10 and 12 April; 29 May; 12 June; 7 August.

Ricard, Matthieu, Published in *L'Infini dans la paume de la main*. © 2000 Nil Editions, Paris: 7 March.

Salzberg, Sharon, From *Lovingkindness. The Revolutionary Art of Happiness*. © 1995 by Sharon Salzberg. Reprinted by arrangement with Shambhala Publications, Inc., Boston, www.shambhala.com: 21 February; 23 October.

Shabkar, Published in *Shabkar, autobiographie d'un yogi tibétain*. © 1998 Editions Albin Michel, Paris: 2, 8 and 29 January; 25 June; 6 August; 25 December.

Shantideva, *A Guide to the Bodhisattva's Way of Life*: 5 and 15 January; 13, 29 and 30 March; 11 April; 14 June; 6 July; 10 and 11 September; 2, 4, 8 and 13–14 October; 1, 22 and 28 November; 6 and 8–9 December.

Sogyal Rinpoche, From *The Tibetan Book of Living and Dying*. © 1993 by Rigpa Fellowship. Reprinted by permission of HarperCollins Publishers Inc., New York and Random House UK Ltd, London: 20–21 and 25 January; 23 February; 2 April; 7 and 31 May; 23 and 24 July; 20 August; 20 September; 14 December.

Photographs copyright © 2003 Olivier Föllmi

This book would not have been possible without the assistance of Anne-Marie Meneux. Texts by Joseph Golstein and Sharon Salzberg was translated by Christian Bruyat. The calligraphy on the endpaper were done by Jigme Douche.

Published in the United States by Stewart, Tabori & Chang
A Company of La Martinière Groupe
115 West 18th Street
New York, NY 10011

Canadian Distribution:
Canadian Manda Group
One Atlantic Avenue, Suite 105
Toronto, Ontario M6K 3E7
Canada

Library of Congress Cataloging-in-Publication Data

Printed in Italy

10 9 8 7 6 5 4 3 2 1

First U.S. Printing

When you are master of your body, word and mind,

you shall rejoice in perfect serenity.

Shabkar